Hands-on Activities
For Exceptional Students

Educational and Pre-Vocational Activities
for Students with Cognitive Delays

By Beverly Thorne

D1379881

Peytral Publications, Inc.
Minnetonka, Minnesota 55345
952-949-8707

Hands-on Activities For Exceptional Students - Educational and Pre-Vocational
Activities for Students with Cognitive Delays
by Beverly Thorne

Published by:

Peytral Publications, Inc.
P.O. Box 1162
Minnetonka, MN 55345
Tel: 952-949-8707
FAX: 952-906-9777

Publisher's Cataloging-in-Publication
(Provided by Quality Books, Inc.)

Thorne, Beverly.
   Hands-on activities for exceptional students :
educational and prevocational activities for students
with cognitive delays / Beverly Thorne. – 1st ed.
   p. cm
   ISBN: 1-890455-31-8

   1. Mentally handicapped children—Education.
2. Creative activities and seatwork.   I. Title.

LC4611.T46 2001   371.9'28
                         QB100-1096

Library of Congress Control Number: 2001 131135

Table of Contents

Preface -- 3

Part I: Vocational Activities

Matching Activities

Activity 1 - Matching Number Cards (2-7 digits)----------------------- 10
Activity 2 - Matching Shape Cards ----------------------------------- 11
Activity 3 - Pen Activity-- 12
Activity 4 - Pencil/Eraser Activity --------------------------------- 13
Activity 5 - Matching & Tying Shoelaces ----------------------------- 14
Activity 6 - Texture Matching Activity ------------------------------ 15
Activity 7 - Hook/Washer Activity ----------------------------------- 16

Sorting Activities

Activity 8 - Sorting Assorted Beads --------------------------------- 17
Activity 9 - Sorting Silverware ------------------------------------- 18
Activity 10 - Sorting Colored Paperclips ------------------------------ 19
Activity 11 - Construction Paper Activity ----------------------------- 20
Activity 12 - Recycling Activity -------------------------------------- 21
Activity 13 - Sorting Numbers & Letters ------------------------------- 22
Activity 14 - Sorting Playing Cards ----------------------------------- 23

Bundling Activities

Activity 15 - Wrapping/Bundling Plastic Flatware----------------------- 24
Activity 16 - Bundling Coffee Stirrers -------------------------------- 25
Activity 17 - Bundling Index Cards ------------------------------------ 26
Activity 18 - Bundling Pencils -- 27
Activity 19 - Bundling Pens --- 28

Assembly Activities

Activity 20 - Hardware Assembly --------------------------------------- 29
Activity 21 - Ball-point Pen Assembly --------------------------------- 30
Activity 22 - Flashlight Assembly ------------------------------------- 31

Bagging/Packaging Activities

Activity 23 - Bagging Plastic Flatware & Condiments ------------------- 32
Activity 24 - Packaging Activity -- 33
Activity 25 - Weighing/Packaging Activity ------------------------------ 34

Various Clerical Activities

Activity 26 - Folding Paper into 1/3's & Stuffing Envelopes ------------ 35
Activity 27 - Stuffing Envelopes -- 37
Activity 28 - Clipping Index Cards --- 38
Activity 29 - Cross-stacking Construction Paper ------------------------- 39
Activity 30 - Hole-Punch Activity -- 40
Activity 31 - Labeling Envelopes --- 41
Activity 32 - Stamping Envelopes -- 42
Activity 33 - Stapling Activity --- 43
Activity 34 - Taping Activity --- 44
Activity 35 - Twine Activity -- 45
Activity 36 - Paper Grid Activity -- 46

Part II: Math Activities

Money Activities

Activity 1 - Coin Matching Activity --------------------------------------- 50
Activity 2 - Penny Counting Activity -------------------------------------- 51
Activity 3 - Nickel Counting Activity ------------------------------------- 52
Activity 4 - Dime Counting Activity --------------------------------------- 53
Activity 5 - Quarter Counting Activity ------------------------------------ 54
Activity 6 - Sorting Paper Money -- 55
Activity 7 - Sorting Plastic Coins --- 56
Activity 8 - Money Bingo -- 57

Counting Activities

Activity 9 - Sequencing Number Cards ----------------------------------- 58
Activity 10 - Matching Number Cards to Set Cards --------------------- 59
Activity 11 - Sequencing Set Cards -- 60
Activity 12 - Counting Activity -- 61
Activity 13 - Tracing /Writing Numbers ----------------------------------- 62
Activity 14 - Writing by 5's -- 63
Activity 15 - Writing by 10's -- 64
Activity 16 - Sequencing by 5's --- 65
Activity 17 - Sequencing by 10's --- 66

Various Math Activities

Activity 18 - Sorting by Place Value --- 67
Activity 19 - Adding Train --- 68
Activity 20 - Clock Face Activity --- 69
Activity 21 - Writing on Clock Face -- 70

Part III: Language/Reading Activities

Alphabet Activities

Activity 1 - ABC Train -- 72
Activity 2 - Writing/Tracing ABC's -- 73
Activity 3 - Sorting Upper/Lowercase Letters-------------------------------- 74
Activity 4 - Sorting Word Cards -- 75
Activity 5 - Sequencing ABC's-- 76
Activity 6 - Alphabetizing Word Cards --------------------------------------- 77

Language Activities

Activity 7 - Sorting Food Groups -- 78
Activity 8 - Sorting Transportation Pictures -------------------------------- 79
Activity 9 - Sorting Clothing Pictures --------------------------------------- 80
Activity 10 - Sorting Object/Action Pictures-------------------------------- 81
Activity 11 - Sorting Boy/Girl Pictures ------------------------------------- 82
Activity 12 - Sorting Man/Woman Pictures--------------------------------- 83
Activity 13 - Matching Pictures to Restroom Signs---------------------- 84
Activity 14 - Sorting Food/Nonfood Pictures ------------------------------ 85
Activity 15 - Sorting Clothing Items -- 86
Activity 16 - Placing Word Cards on Objects----------------------------- 87
Activity 17 - Labeling Parts of the Body ----------------------------------- 88

Appendix

Part I: Vocational Activities Mastery Checklists

Matching Activities (1-7) --- 92
Sorting Activities (8-14) -- 93
Bundling Activities (15-19) -- 94
Assembly Activities (20-22)-- 95
Bagging/Packaging Activities (23-25) --------------------------------------- 96
Various Clerical Activities (26-32)--- 97
Various Clerical Activities (33-36)--- 98

Part II: Math Activities Mastery Checklists

Money Activities (1-8) --- 100
Counting Activities (9-17)-- 101
Various Math Activities (18-21) -- 102

Part III: Language/Reading Activities Mastery Checklists

Alphabet Activities (1-6)--- 104
Language Activities (7-14) --- 105
Language Activities (15-17)--- 106

About the Author

About the Author--- 107

Dedication

To my husband, Bobby, without whose unfailing support and devotion, this book would not have been written.

To my precious daughter, Kristen, whose appearance enabled me to take the opportunity to write this book.

To all my mentors, coworkers and extraordinary students through the years with whom I have been blessed.

To you, the reader, for whom this book was written and to whom I hope helps.

Preface

Why I Wrote This Book

While on a break from teaching after having my first child, I began thinking about a way to share some of the ideas that I used in my classroom. Over several years, we had created quite a wealth of activities designed to be completed independently.

The activities that I came up with to use in my classroom, taught the students a particular skill, as well as teaching them to become more self-sufficient. Since most of my students would be working in some type of supported employment environment, learning to work independently as well as productively was crucial to their survival upon leaving the school. All of the kids were moderate to low-functioning, non-verbal students with significant behavioral problems. Finding a way to just keep them seated and on-task was a big challenge, at times. So, I decided to focus mainly on these objectives and thus created the activities found in this book.

The time spent on vocational preparation activities in my classroom took up the largest part of our school day. The students had to become accustomed to sitting or standing in an area, remaining on-task and focused until their activity was complete. This was the only way they would ever be prepared to work in a sheltered workshop environment for 6-8 hours per day.

You will find that most of the activities listed in this book will fit into a school box or other small, stackable container of your choice. In my classroom, we used small cardboard boxes and called each activity a "workbox." Each workbox was labeled with a colored shape and the students were given a schedule of 4-5 workboxes to complete during the vocational portion of our day. The schedule was made to resemble a poster and was hanging near the shelves containing all of the workboxes. Every morning, I would place 4-5 shapes by each student's name, and that student then knew which workboxes he was responsible for and in what order they were to be completed on that day. It took some time to get the students accustomed to the system, but soon they were able to locate their workboxes and begin working with only verbal or signed prompts.

The system worked so well during the vocational part of our day, that I began using a modified form of workboxes in our math and language hours as well. A few days a week, after the students received direct instruction from either myself or one of my aides, the students would complete a math or language workbox. The math and language activities that I used to reinforce concepts are found in Parts II and III of this book.

These activities were so successful for me that I felt they needed to be shared with other teachers struggling for new ideas as I was. If you choose to incorporate these activities into your schedules, change them up frequently to prevent the students from becoming bored and uncooperative! My hope is that the teachers or caregivers will use these ideas and build on them, coming up with their own activities, too. So, God bless you and good luck!

Part 1:
Vocational Activities

Vocational Activity #1
Matching Number Cards (2-7 digits)

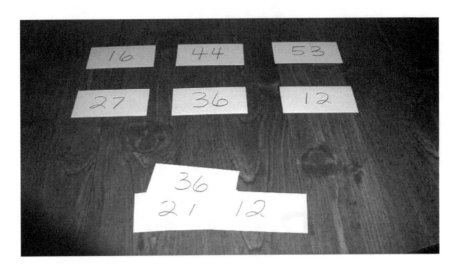

Objective:

Students will be able to match like-numbers. This activity will help the students to increase visual discrimination; improve fine motor skills; sustain attention to task and develop skills to work in a clerical type position.

What you will need:

❋ Index cards

How to prepare the activity:

Divide the pack of index cards in half. On one-half of the deck, write two-digit numbers on each of the cards. On the other half, write the same two-digit numbers to create two matching sets of cards. When making the 3, 4, 5, 6 and 7 digit sets, repeat the above steps, making six separate activities.

Activity:

Shuffle the deck of cards. Ask the student to place one of each number card face up on the table. The student will match the remaining cards in his hand to the corresponding card on the table.

Vocational Activity #2
Matching Shape Cards

Objective:

Students will be able to match like shapes and clip them together. This activity with help the student: increase visual discrimination; improve fine motor skills; prepare the student to work in a clerical environment or supportive employment environment.

What you will need:

* Index cards (25)
* Markers
* Paper clips
* Container for clipped cards

How to prepare the activity:

Divide the index cards into sets of five. Draw one red circle, square, triangle, rectangle and star on each of the five separate cards. Repeat the shapes using a different color each time. When complete provide the student with the stack of cards, some large paper clips and a container to place each set of completed cards.

Activity:

The student will sort through the deck of shape cards, find sets of matching cards and clip the cards together. The student will place completed cards into a container placed to the side of the student's work area.

Vocational Activity #3
Pen Activity

Objective:

Students will match and sort pens by color, for a teacher-specified period of time. This activity will help the student: improve attention to detail; improve visual discrimination; increase fine motor skills; and help to prepare to work in a supportive employment setting.

What you will need:

* Red, blue, green and black ink pens with matching caps
* Sorting tray

How to prepare the activity:

Remove the caps from the ink pens and place the pens and the caps into a container. Place the container of pens and pen caps and a sorting tray in the student's work area.

Activity:

The student will match the colored cap to the corresponding colored pen. The student will then sort the pens into sorting trays.

Vocational Activity #4
Pencil/Eraser Activity

Objective:

Students will match and sort pencils, for a teacher-specified period of time. This activity will help the student: improve attention to detail; improve visual discrimination; increase attention to task; increase fine motor skills and help prepare the student to work in a supportive employment type setting.

What you will need:

* Colored pencil top erasers (several boxes)
* Pencils (several packages)
* Sorting tray

How to prepare the activity:

Place the erasers and the pencils into a container. Place this container and a sorting tray in the student's work area.

Activity:

The student will place erasers on the pencils and then sort the pencils by eraser color into sorting trays.

Vocational Activity #5
Matching & Tying Shoelaces

Objective:

Students will match and sort assorted shoelaces, for a teacher-specified period of time. This activity will help the student: increase visual discrimination; improve fine motor skills; and increase attention to task.

What you will need:

* ❋ Several different types of shoelaces*
* ❋ Container to place matched shoelaces

   * *You can find laces with many different designs on them.*

How to prepare the activity:

Mix up all of the shoelaces and place them into a container. Provide the student with a container in his workspace to place the pairs of shoelaces.

Activity:

The student will sort through the shoelaces, find a matching pair, tie the laces into a knot or bow and place the finished pairs into the container.

Vocational Activity #6
Texture Matching Activity

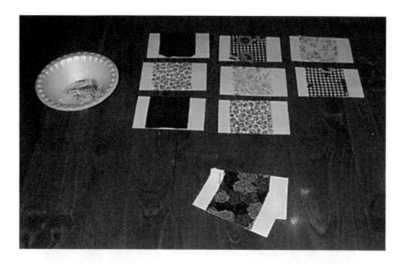

Objective:

Students will match like-textured swatches, through visual and tactile means. This activity will help the student: increase visual and sensory discrimination; improve fine motor skills; and sustain attention to task.

What you will need:

* Wallpaper samples
* Index cards
* Paper clips
* Container for matched samples

How to prepare the activity:

Cut numerous sets of wallpaper samples and affix the samples to index cards. Place the samples, paper clips and a container for matched sets in the student's work area.

Activity:

The student will sort through the stack of wallpaper samples and find matching sets. The student will clip the samples together using a paper clip and place the set into the container.

Vocational Activity #7
Hook/Washer Activity

Objective:

Students will match washers to similarly sized hooks. This activity will help the student: increase visual discrimination; increase fine motor skills; and help prepare to work in a supportive employment setting.

What you will need:

* Screw-in hooks (several different sizes)
* Washers (coordinate size w/hook sizes)
* Small piece of 1" thick plywood (approximately 1' by 1')

How to prepare the activity:

Randomly screw the hooks into the plywood. Place the "hook board" and washers in the student's work environment.

Activity:

The student will hang a washer on the hook of similar size. The student will continue until all of the hooks are filled.

Vocational Activity #8
Sorting Assorted Beads

Objective:

Students will sort beads, by color or shape. This activity will help the student: increase visual discrimination; increase attention to detail; and improve fine motor skills.

What you will need:

* Big bag of mixed colored beads
* Container for the beads
* Sorting tray

*Note: This can be made into many separate activities. You can find opaque, clear or metallic beads. You can also use different varieties of beads, for example: pony beads, tri-beads, star-shaped beads, and square beads.

How to prepare the activity:

Pour the contents of the bag into a container of your choice. Each variety of beads makes another activity.

Activity:

To help the student get started, place one bead of each of color into one of the sections of the sorting tray. The student will sort the beads according to color or shape.

Vocational Activity #9
Sorting Silverware

Objective:

Students will sort spoons, forks, and knives into the appropriate silverware containers. This activity helps the student: increase visual discrimination; sustain attention to task; and prepare the student to work in a cafeteria setting;

What you will need:

* Plastic spoons, forks and knives
* Sorting bins

How to prepare the activity:

Mix up the different pieces of plastic silverware and place them into a large container such as a shoebox. Also provide three sorting bins for the student to sort the silverware.

Activity:

The student will sort the silverware into containers marked for spoons, forks and knives.

Vocational Activity #10
Sorting Colored Paper Clips

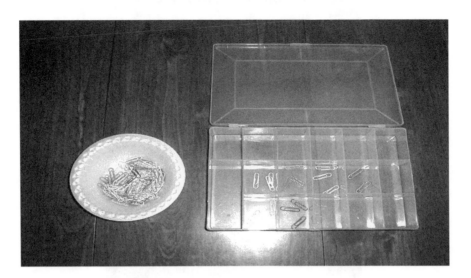

Objective:

Students will sort colored paper clips. This activity will help the student: discriminate between both color and size; improve fine motor skills; increase attention to task and prepare the student to work in a supported employment setting;

What you will need:

* ❋ Colored paper clips (both large and small)
* ❋ Sorting tray

How to prepare the activity:

Pour all of the colored paper clips into a container. Place the container of paper clips and a sorting tray in the student's work area.

Activity:

The student will sort the paper clips, by color, into a sorting tray. If you have two sizes of paper clips, the student may then sort the individual groups of colored paper clips into groups of large and small paper clips.

Vocational Activity #11
Construction Paper Activity

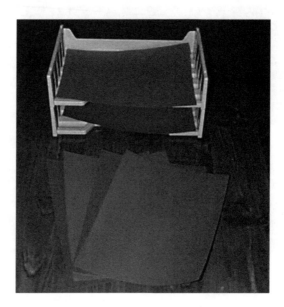

Objective:

Students will sort packages of construction paper into the appropriately colored piles. This activity will help the student: increase fine motor skills; increase attention to task; and help prepare the student to work in a clerical type setting.

What you will need:

* ❋ Construction paper (several packages)
* ❋ Stacking paper trays*

You will need one paper tray for each color of construction paper.

How to prepare the activity:

Place the packages of construction paper and the stacked paper trays in the student's work area.

Activity:

The student will sort the construction paper by color into the stacked paper trays.

Vocational Activity #12
Recycling Activity

Objective:

The student will sort and separate newspapers, by placing them into the appropriately marked bins. This activity will help the student: increase visual discrimination; increase attention to task; and increase social skills.

What you will need:

* Donated newspapers
* Plastic bins to sort the newspaper into

How to prepare the activity:

Label two large plastic containers: one container for colored sale papers and the second for printed newspapers. For non-readers, affix a sample to the front of the bin.

Activity:

The student will sort through the newspaper, separating the sale papers from the printed newspaper, and place them into the appropriate bins. Explain to the student that sale papers are not recyclable, and must be separated from the newspapers. You may also ask the student to collect the old newspapers, on a daily basis, from the main office, media center and the staff lounge.

Vocational Activity #13
Sorting Numbers & Letters

Objective:

Students will sort index cards by placing them into either letter or number stacks. This activity will help the student: increase visual discrimination; distinguish between numbers and letters; and increase attention to detail.

What you will need:

* Index cards

How to prepare the activity:

Divide a package of index cards in half. On one-half of the deck, write various upper or lowercase letters. On the other half of the deck, write various one and two digit numbers. Shuffle the deck.

Activity:

The student will sort the cards into two piles: one for letters and one for numbers.

Vocational Activity #14
Sorting Playing Cards

Objective:

Students will sort decks of cards, either by color, suit or numerical value, by placing them into the appropriate stacks. This activity will help the student: increase visual discrimination skills; improve number recognition; and sustain attention to task;

What you will need:

* Playing cards

How to prepare the activity:

Shuffle the cards and place one card from each suit on the table in front of the student.

Activity:

There are several options for this activity:

* The student will sort the cards into four piles: one for hearts, diamonds, clubs and spades.
* The student will sort the cards into to piles: red and black.
* The student will sort the cards according to their numeric value.

Vocational Activity #15
Wrapping/Bundling Plastic Flatware

Objective:

Students will wrap/bundle plastic flatware with napkins. This activity will help the student: increase visual discrimination; increase fine motor skills; gain experience with a multiple step task; and help prepare the student to work in a cafeteria type setting.

What you will need:

* Plastic spoons, forks and knives
* Paper napkins
* Strips of paper and a glue stick
* Container for wrapped silverware

How to prepare the activity:

Presort the silverware into individual bins. Place the bins in the student's work area. Also provide a stack of paper napkins, paper strips and a glue stick. The student will also need a container to place the wrapped silverware.

Activity:

The student will lay a napkin in the table and place one fork, one spoon and one knife on the napkin. The student will wrap the napkin around the silverware. The student wraps a strip of paper around the bundle and secures it with a dot of glue.

Vocational Activity #16
Bundling Coffee-Stirrers

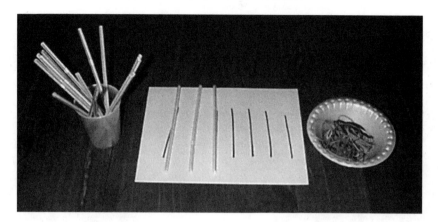

Objective:

Students will bundle a predetermined number of coffee stirrers, by placing them on a pre-drawn template and wrapping them with a rubber band. This activity will help students: increase counting and matching skills; increase fine motor skills; reinforce the concept of left to right; complete multiple step tasks; and help prepare the student for a supportive employment work setting.

What you will need:

* Wooden coffee stirrers
* Rubber bands
* Container to place completed bundles

How to prepare the activity:

Working from left-to-right, place the coffee stirrers, the rubber bands and a container for the completed bundles in the student's work area. Directly in front of the student, place a sheet of paper with 10 vertically drawn lines. This model will help the student count the correct number of stirrers.

Activity:

The student will place one coffee stirrer per line on the model template. Upon completion the student will gather the stirrers together and wrap a rubber band securely around the bundle. The bundle is then placed into a container.

Vocational Activity #17
Bundling Index Cards

Objective:

Students will bundle a predetermined number of index cards and wrap them with a rubber band. This activity will help the student: increase counting skills; increase fine motor skills; sustain attention to task; and help the student to prepare to work in a supportive employment setting.

What you will need:

* ❋ Index cards
* ❋ Rubber bands

How to prepare the activity:

Place four stacks (or more) of index cards and a container of rubber bands in the student's work area.

Activity:

The student will take one card from each stack, tap the index cards on the table to align them, wrap a rubber band around the set and place the bundle in a container.

Vocational Activity #18
Bundling Pencils

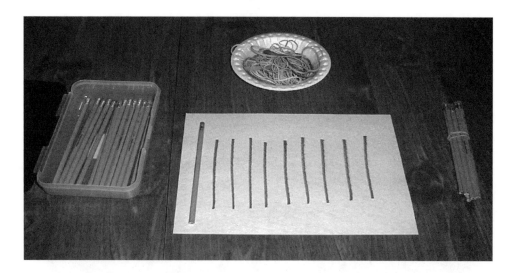

Objective:

The student will bundle a predetermined number of pencils, and wrap them with a rubber band. This activity will help the student: increase one-to-one correspondence; fine motor skills; complete multiple step activities; and help prepare the student to work in a supportive employment environment.

What you will need:

* Pencils (or colored pencils for more advanced students)
* Rubber bands
* Container to place completed bundles

How to prepare the activity:

Working from left-to-right, place the pencils, the rubber bands and a container for the completed bundles in the student's work area. Create a template with vertically drawn lines and place it in front of where the student will work. This will serve as a guide to help the student count the correct number of pencils.

Activity:

The student will place one pencil on each line of the template. If using colored pencils the student will bundle a predetermined number of same color pencils. The student then gathers the pencils together and wraps a rubber band securely around the bundle. The bundle is placed into the container.

Vocational Activity #19
Bundling Pens

Objective:

Students will select a specified number of pens and wrap them with a rubber band. This activity will help the student increase: increase visual discrimination (if using colored pens); increase fine motor skills; and become proficient with multiple step tasks.

What you will need:

* Pens (one color or multiple colors)
* Rubber bands
* Container to place completed bundles

How to prepare the activity:

Working from left-to-right, place the pens, the rubber bands and a container for the completed bundles in the student's work area. Directly in front of where the student will be sitting, place the template with the predetermined number of vertical lines. This will serve as a guide for student.

Activity:

The student will place one pen on each of the vertical lines. The student gathers the pens together, wraps a rubber band securely around the bundle and places the bundle into a container.

Vocational Activity #20
Hardware Assembly

Objective:

Student will complete 3-piece hardware assemblies. This activity will help the student: increase fine motor skills; sustain attention while completing a multiple step activity; and help prepare the student for a supportive employment setting.

What you will need:

* Bin filled with bolts
* Bin filled with washers
* Bin filled with nuts
* Container for assembled hardware

How to prepare the activity:

Place the bolt bin, washer bin, and nut bin from left to right in the student's work area. Also place container for assembled hardware to the right of the bins.

Activity:

The student will take a bolt, washer, and nut from each of the bins and assemble the three pieces of hardware. The student places the completed hardware into the container for completed assemblies.

Vocational Activity #21
Ball-point Pen Assembly

Objective:

Students will assemble ballpoint pens by following steps. This activity will help the student: increase fine motor skills; follow sequential directions; complete a multiple step task; and increase skills needed to work in a supportive employment setting.

What you will need:

* ❋ Box of ballpoint pens
* ❋ Bins for pen parts (4)
* ❋ Container for completed assemblies

How to prepare the activity:

Disassemble the ballpoint pens. Place the following into 4 separate bins: ink cartridges, springs, top-half, and bottom–half of the pen. Place the bins and a container for completed pens in the student's work area.

Activity:

The student will assemble the ballpoint pens by completing the following steps:

a) take the one spring from the 1st bin
b) place the spring on the ink cartridge
c) place the cartridge in the bottom-half of the pen
d) screw the top-half of the pen onto the bottom-half

Vocational Activity #22
Flashlight Assembly

Objective:

Students will reinforce basic assembly skills. This activity will help the student: follow multiple step directions; increase on-task behavior; and help prepare the student to work in a supportive employment environment.

What you will need:

* Flashlights
* "D"-cell batteries
* Bins for flashlight parts (3)
* Container for completed assembled flashlights

How to prepare the activity:

Disassemble the flashlights and place the top-halves of the flashlights, the bottom-halves of the flashlights and the batteries in separate bins. Place the bins and a container for completed flashlights in the student's work area.

Activity:

The student will assemble the flashlights by completing the following steps:

a) take a bottom-half from the 1st bin
b) place two batteries in the bottom-half
c) screw the top-half onto the bottom-half

Vocational Activity #23
Bagging Plastic Flatware & Condiments

Objective:

Students will assemble packets of flatware and condiments. This activity will help the student: follow multiple step directions; be consistent when packaging items; and help prepare students to work in a cafeteria setting.

What you will need:

* Plastic spoons, forks, and knives
* Paper napkins
* Packets of salt and pepper
* Zipper bags (snack size)
* Container for bagged flatware

How to prepare the activity:

Sort flatware into individual bins and place them in the student's work area. Also provide a stack of paper napkins, salt and pepper packets and zipper bags. The student will also need a container to place the bagged silverware.

Activity:

The student will place one each of the following into a zipper bag: fork, spoon, knife, salt and pepper packet, and napkin. The student places the completed bags into a container.

Vocational Activity #24
Packaging Activity

Objective:

Students will package 3-5 objects into zipper bags. This activity will help the student: increase counting skills; increase fine motor skills; establish left-right sequencing; and help to prepare the student to work in a supportive employment setting.

What you will need:

* 3-5 Bins filled with items of your choice*
* Zipper bags
* Container for bagged items

   Tokens, screws, nuts, washers, counting cubes, etc

How to prepare the activity:

Place the bins and zipper bags from left to right in front of the student. Provide a container for the student to place the completed bags.

Activity:

The student will take one item from each of the bins, working from left to right. The student places each item into the zipper bag. The student seals the bag and places it into a container.

Vocational Activity #25
Weighing/Packaging Activity

Objective:

Students will weigh and package specific items. This activity will help students: increase proficiency with multiple step tasks; increase accuracy by determining specific weights; and help to prepare the student for a supportive employment setting.

What you will need:

* Bin filled with item of your choice*
* Zipper bags
* Kitchen scale w/tray
* Container for bagged items

    *Slightly heavy items such as: screws, nuts, washers, bolts

How to prepare the activity:

Place the bin, kitchen scale, zipper bags and container for bagged items in the workspace.

Activity:

The student will place items into the tray until the items weigh approximately one pound. The student empties the contents of the tray into a zipper bag, seals the bag and places it into the container. Note: If the student has difficulty determining the one-pound mark place a sticker on the area.

Vocational Activity #26
Folding Paper into 1/3's & Stuffing Envelopes

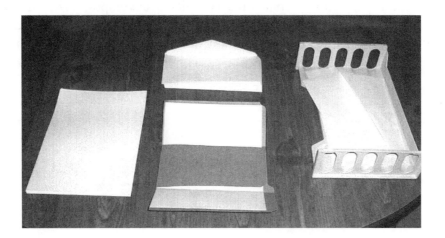

Objective:

Students will fold paper into thirds by using a paper-folding jig. This activity will help the student: increase proficiency in multiple step tasks; and help the student prepare to work in a clerical position.

What you will need:

* Manila folder
* Letter-sized paper
* Legal-sized envelopes
* Paper tray

How to prepare the activity:

To make a paper-folding "jig," follow the steps below:

1) Draw two lines on the front of the manila folder, dividing the front (lengthwise) into thirds.
2) Cut along the lines you have drawn, stopping at the crease of the folder.
3) Cut along the crease of the folder, cutting up for the top line and down for the bottom line. You will then have one strip left in the center of the folder.
4) Fold the manila folder into thirds. The strip on the front of folder will be in the center of the fold.

Activity:

Give the student a stack of paper, a stack of envelopes and the paper-folding jig. Also provide a paper tray to place the completed envelopes. The student places each sheet of paper onto the jig, folding the jig around the paper into thirds. Once the student has folded the paper, the student inserts it into an envelope and places it into the paper tray.

Vocational Activity #27
Stuffing Envelopes

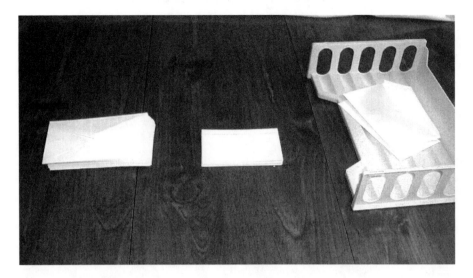

Objective:

Students will place sheets of paper into letter-sized envelopes. This activity will help the student: increase fine motor skills; become proficient with multiple step procedures; and help prepare the student to work in a clerical type environment.

What you will need:

* Letter-sized envelopes
* Index cards (3 x 5 size)
* Paper tray

How to prepare the activity:

Line up the stack of index cards, envelopes and paper tray in the student's work area.

Activity:

The student will place each index card into an envelope. Once inserted the student may either tuck the flap into the envelope to close it. The final envelope is placed in the paper tray.

Vocational Activity #28
Clipping Index Cards

Objective:

Students will count and clip together a predetermined number of index cards. This activity will help the student: increase counting skills; refine fine motor skills; and understand the concept of left/right.

What you will need:

* Index cards
* Paper clips
* Container for finished product

How to prepare the activity:

Place a stack of index cards and a container of paper clips in the student's workspace.

Activity:

The student will count out two index cards* (or whatever the predetermined number) and clip them together in the upper left-hand corner.

*If the student is having difficulty counting two cards create a template with the outline of two index cards. The student places can place the two index cards onto the template before clipping them together.

Vocational Activity #29
Cross-stacking Construction Paper

Objective:

Students will cross-stack sets of colored construction paper. This activity will help the student: increase fine motor skills; learn collating skills; establish left to right sequence; understand the concepts of under and over; and help prepare the student to work in a clerical environment.

What you will need:

* Construction paper (4-5 colors)

How to prepare the activity:

Line stacks of previously sorted construction paper, from left to right in the student's work area.

Activity:

The student will take one piece of construction paper from the first stack. Working from left to right, the student places the second sheet under the first sheet. When complete demonstrate how to tap the edges of the paper on the table to align the papers. When aligned the student will place the stack to the side of the workspace. Repeat the above process, cross-stacking each successive set of papers.

Vocational Activity #30
Hole-Punch Activity

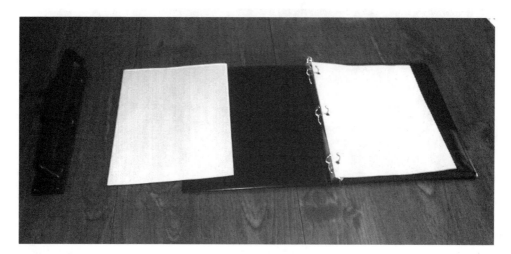

Objective:

Students will be able to use a hole punch to prepare sheets for placement in a 3-ring binder. This activity will help the student: use a simple office tool; follow a multiple step task; understand the concept of left/right; and help prepare the student to work in a clerical setting.

What you will need:

* Letter-sized paper
* Hole punch – set fit the binder
* Three ring binder

How to prepare the activity:

Working from left-to-right, place the stack of paper, the hole punch and an opened notebook in the student's work area.

Activity:

The student will take one piece of paper from the stack, place it into the hole punch and make the holes in the paper. Then the student will place the paper face down onto the left-hand side of the opened notebook. The student will continue for a teacher-specified period of time.

Vocational Activity #31
Labeling Envelopes

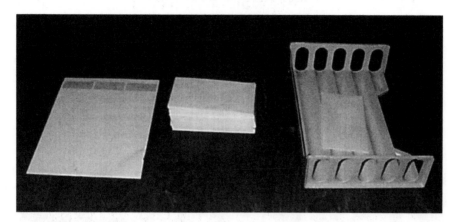

Objective:

Students will place return address labels in the proper space of the envelope. This activity will help the student: reinforce left and right; increase fine motor development; and help prepare the student to work in a clerical setting.

What you will need:

* Envelopes
* Return address labels
* Paper tray

How to prepare the activity:

Place a stack of envelopes, a box of labels and a paper tray in the student's work area.

Activity:

The student will peel the address label from the sheet. The student applies the address label to the upper left-hand corner of the envelope and places the envelope in the paper tray.

Once the student becomes proficient with the return address labels, continue the procedure with the main address label until proficient. When the student is proficient in the skill have the student apply the skill with school mailings.

Vocational Activity #32
Stamping Envelopes

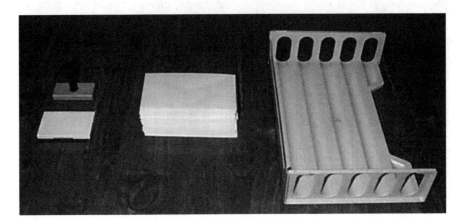

Objective:

Students will stamp envelopes in the address space of an envelope, using an address stamp. This activity will help the student: become familiar with using a stamp and inkpad; increase understanding of left/right; help prepare the student for work in a clerical setting.

What you will need:

* Envelopes
* Address stamp and inkpad
* Paper tray

How to prepare the activity:

Place a stack of envelopes, an address stamp, inkpad and a paper tray in the student's work area.

Activity:

The student will stamp the address into the upper left-hand corner of the envelope and place the envelope in the paper tray. You may want to place a sheet of construction paper under the envelopes to avoid ink on the tabletop.

Vocational Activity #33
Stapling Activity

Objective:

Students will staple a specified number of sheets together in the upper left-hand corner of the paper stack. This activity will help the student: learn to use a simple office tool; distinguish between left and right; and help the student prepare for work in a clerical setting.

What you will need:

* Letter-sized paper
* Stapler
* Paper tray

How to prepare the activity:

Place two stacks of paper, a stapler and a paper tray in the student's work area.

Activity:

The student will take one sheet of paper from each of the two stacks of paper, tap the paper on the table to align the edges and staple the paper on the upper left-hand side of the paper. The student places the stapled paper into a paper tray when complete.

Vocational Activity #34
Taping Activity

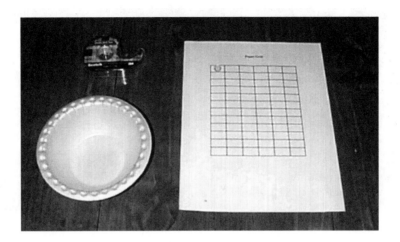

Objective:

Students affix buttons to a grid using double-sided tape. This activity will help the student: increase fine motor control; follow multiple step directions; and increase attention to task.

What you will need:

* Double-sided tape
* Buttons (or a substitute item)
* Scissors
* Paper grid

How to prepare the activity:

Place a container of buttons, scissors, double-sided tape and a paper grid in the student's work area.

Activity:

The student tears off a button-sized piece of tape, peels off the paper and affixes the tape to the button. Next the student peels the paper from the other side of the tape and sticks the button inside one of the squares on the paper grid. The student should continue until the grid is completely filled with buttons.

Vocational Activity #35
Twine Activity

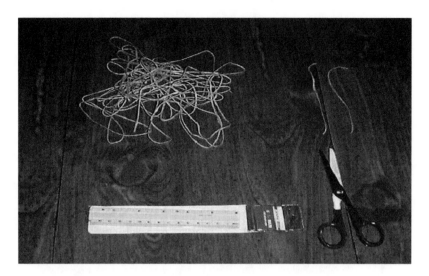

Objective:

Students will measure and cut string into specified lengths. This activity will help the student: increase basic understanding of measurement; improve fine motor skills; and reinforce counting skills.

What you will need:

* Ball of twine
* Scissors
* 6 " Ruler

How to prepare the activity:

Place the ball of twine, a ruler, and a pair of scissors in the student's work area.

Activity:

The student will measure a piece of twine 6" long (the length of the ruler) and cut the twine. The twine may be piled into groups to reinforce counting skills. The student continues until he has cut a specified number of pieces or for a specific amount of time.

Vocational Activity #36
Paper Grid Activity

Objective:

Students will affix squares of construction paper onto a grid using glue. This activity will help the student: increase fine motor skills; and increase attention to task.

What you will need:

* Paper Grid (see p. 47)
* Small squares of construction paper (cut to fit squares)
* Stick or liquid glue

How to prepare the activity:

Cut up small squares of construction paper (a small box full). Place the box of squares, the glue and the paper grid in front of where the student will be working.

Activity:

The student will glue the paper squares into the squares on the paper grid, making sure that the construction paper squares do not touch the lines on the grid. If you would like for the student to strengthen his ability to follow directions, then dot a color with the tip of a marker into each of the squares on the grid. Have the student choose the matching color from the box of paper squares and glue it in the appropriate grid.

Paper Grid

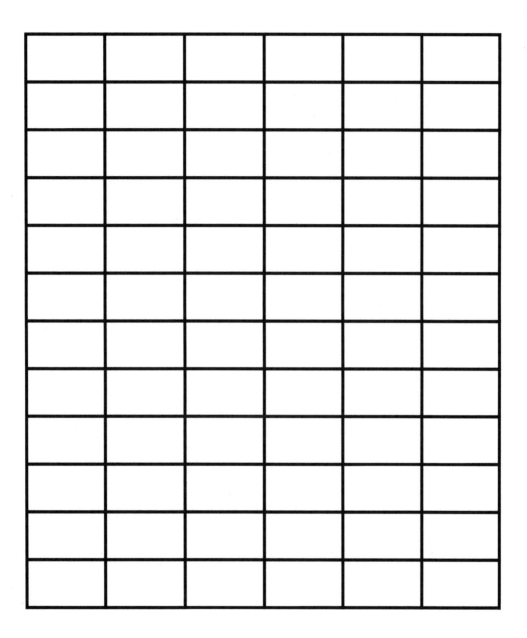

Part II: Math Activities

Math Activity #1
Coin Matching Activity

Objective:

Students will sort and match coins to a teacher-made, stamped template sheet. This activity will help students recognize and discriminate between various denominations of coins.

What you will need:

* ⁜ Plastic coins (Pennies, Nickels, Dimes and Quarters)
* ⁜ Coin stamps
* ⁜ Inkpad
* ⁜ Construction paper

How to prepare the activity:

Using the coin stamps, create the stamp sheets. Select one coin, perhaps the penny stamp, and stamp enough rows to fill a sheet of construction paper. Make three additional stamp sheets, using the dime, nickel and quarter stamps.

To prepare the activity for the student, place a container of plastic coins and one of the stamp sheets in front of where the student will be sitting.

Activity:

The student will choose the correct coins to match the stamp sheet. The student will place the coins over the stamps on the coin sheet. When the student has completed the first stamp sheet, have him move on to the next one.

Math Activity #2
Penny Counting Activity

Objective:

Students will count the appropriate number of coins into cups marked with money values. This activity will help the student: understand the value of one penny; reinforce counting by ones.

What you will need:

* Plastic penny coins
* Clear plastic cups
* Marker

How to prepare the activity:

Using the marker, write a specific amount on the side of each of the cups. (See above diagram.) If you are only working on 1-10 cents, then use only the numbers 1-10. If the student needs additional support counting – provide a numberline.

To prepare the activity for the student, place the cups in front of the student, along with a container of plastic pennies.

Activity:

The student will look at the amount written on the first cup and drops that number of pennies in the cup. The student continues on to the next cup and fills it accordingly. The student will continue until all of the cups have been correctly filled.

Math Activity #3
Nickel Counting Activity

Objective:

Students will count the appropriate number of coins into cups marked with money values. This activity will help the student: recognize the value of five cents; reinforce counting by fives.

What you will need:

* ❋ Plastic nickel coins
* ❋ Clear plastic cups
* ❋ Marker

How to prepare the activity:

Using the marker, write a specific amount on the side of each cup, using increments of five. If the student is working on amounts between 5-50 cents, you will need 10 cups. If the student needs additional help counting by fives, provide a counting strip to the student.

To prepare the activity for the student, place the cups in front of the student, along with a container of plastic nickels.

Activity:

The student will look at the amount written on the first cup and drop the nickels in the cup while counting by fives. The student goes on to the next cup and fills it accordingly.

Math Activity #4
Dime Counting Activity

Objective:

Students will count the appropriate number of coins into cups marked with money values. This activity will help the student: recognize the value of a dime; reinforce counting by tens.

What you will need:

* Plastic dime coins
* Clear plastic cups
* Marker

How to prepare the activity:

Using the marker, write a specific amount on the side of each of the cups. (See diagram.) When working with amounts between 10-50 cents, five cups will be used. If the student needs additional help counting by tens, provide a counting strip to the student.

To prepare the activity for the student, place the cups in front of the student, along with a container of plastic dimes.

Activity:

The student will look at the amount written on the first cup and drop the dimes into the cup, while counting by tens. The student continues to the second cup and fills it accordingly. The student will continue until all of the cups have been correctly filled.

Math Activity #5
Quarter Counting Activity

Objective:

Students will count the appropriate number of coins into cups marked with money values. This activity will help the student: recognize the value of a quarter; reinforce counting by twenty-five.

What you will need:

* ❋ Plastic quarter coins
* ❋ Clear plastic cups
* ❋ Marker

How to prepare the activity:

Using the marker, write a specific amount on the side of each of the cups. (See diagram above.) If the student needs additional help counting by twenty-five, provide a counting strip to the student.

To prepare the activity for the student, place the cups in front of the student, along with a container of plastic quarters.

Activity:

The student will look at the amount written on the first cup and drop the corresponding number of quarters into the cup. The student goes on to the next cup and fills it accordingly. The student will continue until all of the cups have been correctly filled.

Math Activity #6
Sorting Paper Money

Objective:

Students will sort paper money, by denomination, into the appropriately marked stack. This activity will help the student: recognize the various denominations of paper money; increase visual discrimination skills.

What you will need:

* Paper money (ones, fives, tens and twenties)
* Envelopes (4)

How to prepare the activity:

Write the denominations of $1.00, $5.00, $10.00 and $20.00 on each of the envelopes. Shuffle the paper money. Place the stack of money and the four envelopes in the area where the student will be working.

Activity:

The student will sort the money into four piles: ones, tens, fives and twenties. When the money is sorted, the student will place the paper bills into the corresponding envelope.

Math Activity #7
Sorting Plastic Coins

Objective:

Students will sort coins, by value, into the appropriately marked containers. This activity will help the student: increase fine motor skills; increase visual discrimination skills

What you will need:

* Plastic coins (pennies, nickels, dimes and quarters)
* Sorting bins (4)

How to prepare the activity:

Put all of the coins into one container. Provide four additional bins for the student to sort the coins.

Activity:

The student will sort the coins into four bins: pennies, nickels, dimes and quarters.

Math Activity #8
Money BINGO

Objective:

Students will strengthen matching and money counting skills by playing Money Bingo.

What you will need:

* Construction paper
* Plastic money coins

How to prepare the activity:

Make a bingo board by dividing the paper into nine squares and writing monetary value in each of the squares. Place the board and the plastic coins in the student's area.

Activity:

The teacher (or student helper) will call out an amount of change. The student will find the amount on his bingo board, and place the correct amount of change in the square. Game continues until one of the students win. If they student is playing with a "student helper", the game ends when the board is completed.

Math Activity #9
Sequencing Number Cards

Objective:

Students will correctly sequence number cards. This activity will help the student: increase fine motor control; reinforce counting by ones; reinforce number recognition.

What you will need:

* Index cards
* Marker

How to prepare the activity:

Using the index cards, number the cards in chronological order. The numbers used will depend upon the student's level of performance. If the student experiences difficulty, provide a numberline.

Activity:

The student will sequence the cards in chronological order. Expand on the activity by asking the student what number comes "before" or "after" a specific number.

Math Activity #10
Matching Number Cards to Set Cards

Objective:

Students will correctly match the cards the written number cards to the cards displaying the number sets. This activity will help the student: reinforce the concept of numbers; understand the relationship between numbers and symbols.

What you will need:

* Index Cards
* Marker

How to prepare the activity:

Divide the index cards into two piles. On one set of cards, write the numbers 1-10, or 1-20 depending on what you are working on. On the second set of cards, draw the sets (using shapes) to match the number cards you have made. Place the number cards face up in the student's work area and place the set deck in front of the student.

Activity:

The student will match the set cards to the number cards, by placing the appropriate set card face up on the number card.

Math Activity #11
Sequencing Set Cards

Objective:

Students will sequence set cards.   This activity will help the student: reinforce counting; increase visual discrimination skills.

What you will need:

* Index cards
* Marker

How to prepare the activity:

Using the index cards, draw the sets 1-20* on each of the cards.

Depending on which set of numbers you are working on. If working on the sets 1-50, for example, then make the set of cards accordingly.

Activity:

The student will sequence the set cards, 1-20.

Math Activity #12
Counting Activity

Objective:

Students will count the correct number of manipulatives into containers marked with specific numbers. This activity will help the student: increase fine motor skills; reinforce the concept of numerical value; increase ability to perform multiple step tasks.

What you will need:

* Manipulatives
* Clear plastic cups
* Marker

How to prepare the activity:

Using the marker, write a specific amount on the side of each of the cups. (See diagram) If you are only working on the numbers 1-10, then use only those numbers. If you are working on the numbers 1-20, then use the numbers 1-20, and so on.

To prepare the activity for the student, place the cups in front of the student, along with a container of manipulatives.

Activity:

The student will look at the number written on the first cup and drop that number of manipulatives in the cup. The student goes on to the next cup, and fills it accordingly. The student will continue until all of the cups have been correctly filled.

Math Activity #13
Tracing/Writing Numbers

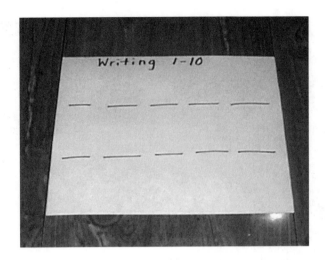

Objective:

Students will write or trace the numbers 1-10, in the correct order. This activity will help the student: increase fine motor skills;

What you will need:

* Construction paper
* Clear contact paper
* Marker
* Dry erase marker
* Paper towels

How to prepare the activity:

Using the construction paper, draw 10 spaces if working on 1-10. If the student has fine motor difficulty, make another worksheet with the numbers 1-10 written on the page, so the student can practice tracing the numbers. Cover the worksheet with clear contact paper. Place the worksheet, paper towels and a dry erase marker in the student's work area.

Activity:

The student will write or trace the numbers 1-10 in the spaces provided.

Math Activity #14
Writing by 5's

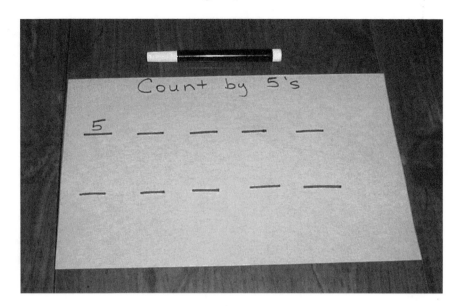

Objective:

Students will write numbers, by 5's, in the correct sequence. This activity help the student: reinforce counting by fives; increase fine motor skills.

What you will need:

* Construction paper
* Clear contact paper
* Marker
* Dry erase marker
* Paper towels

How to prepare the activity:

Using the construction paper, draw 10 spaces if working on 5-50 (worksheet A), and 20 spaces if working on 5-100 (worksheet B). Cover the worksheet with clear contact paper. Place the worksheet, paper towels and a dry erase marker in the student's work area.

Activity:

Counting by 5's, the student will write the numbers 5-50, in the spaces provided on worksheet A, and the numbers 5-100, in the spaces provided on worksheet B.

Math Activity #15
Writing by 10's

Objective:

Students will write numbers, by 10's, in the correct sequence. This activity will help the student: reinforce counting by tens; help increase fine motor skills.

What you will need:

* Construction paper
* Clear contact paper
* Marker
* Dry erase marker
* Paper towels

How to prepare the activity:

Using the construction paper, draw 10 spaces if working on 10-100. Cover the worksheet with clear contact paper. Place the worksheet, paper towels and a dry erase marker in the student's work area.

Activity:

Counting by 10's, the student will write the numbers 10-100, in the spaces provided.

Math Activity #16
Sequencing by 5's

Objective:

Students will sequence number cards by 5's, in the correct sequence. This activity will help the student: reinforce counting by fives.

What you will need:

* Index cards
* Marker

How to prepare the activity:

Using the index cards, write each of the numbers 5-50 on each of the index cards.

Activity:

The student will sequence the cards by 5's (5,10, 15, 20, etc).

Math Activity #17
Sequencing by 10's

Objective:

Students will sequence number cards by 10's, in the correct sequence. This activity will help the student: reinforce counting by tens.

What you will need:

* Index cards
* Marker

How to prepare the activity:

Using the index cards, write each of the numbers 10-100 on each of the index cards.

Activity:

The student will sequence the cards by 10's (10, 20, 30, etc).

Math Activity #18
Sorting by Place Value

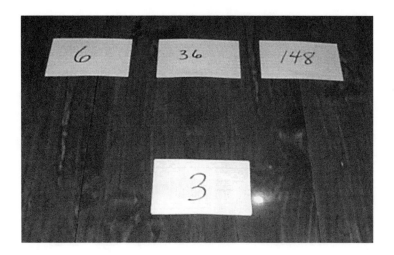

Objective:

Students will sort number cards by place value. This activity will help the student: understand the concept of place value.

What you will need:

* Index cards
* Marker

How to prepare the activity:

Divide the index cards into three stacks. One the first stack, write various one-digit numbers, on the second stack write various two-digit numbers, and on the third stack write various three-digit numbers. Shuffle all of the cards and place the deck in front of the student.

Activity:

The student will sort the cards into three piles by place value: ones, tens and hundreds.

Math Activity #19
Adding Train

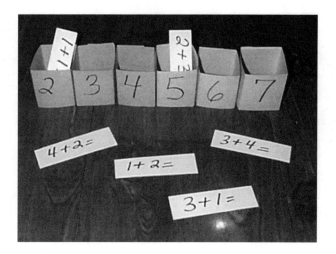

Objective:

Students will strengthen addition skills by matching simple addition problems to the correct sum.   This activity will help the student: reinforce the concepts of numbers; reinforce the concept of simple addition.

What you will need:

* Empty milk cartons (from the cafeteria)
* Index cards (I used neon, for fun)
* Marker
* Stapler

How to prepare the activity:

Cut the top off of all the milk cartons. Cut index cards to wrap around the index cards and staple them on securely. Next, staple all of the milk cartons together to resemble a train. Write a number on each of the cartons. Using the index cards you have left, cut the cards in half, lengthwise. Write an addition problem on each of the cards (2+1=). Place the "Addition Train" and the addition problem cards in front of the student.

Activity:

The student will select an addition problem from the top of the stack and solve the addition problem. The student then places the addition card into the carton with the correct answer written on it.

Math Activity #20
Clock Face Activity

Objective:

Students will place the numbers 1-12, in the correct spaces, on a blank clock face. This activity will help the student: become familiar with the face clock; place numbers in chronological order.

What you will need:

* Poster board
* Marker
* Velcro
* Clear contact paper/laminator

How to prepare the activity:

Cut a piece of poster board approximately 12" by 12". Draw a blank clock face on the poster paper and cover the clock face with clear contact paper. Place a small piece of Velcro where each of the numbers 1-12 would be on a clock face. Next, cut twelve small squares from the remaining poster paper, write the numbers 1-12 on each of the squares, and cover the squares with contact paper. Place a piece of Velcro on the back of each of the squares and you are ready to go!

Activity:

The student will place the numbers 1-12 in the correct order on the blank clock face.

Math Activity #21
Writing on Clock Face

Objective:

Students will write the numbers 1-12, in the correct spaces, on a blank clock face.

What you will need:

* Poster board
* Marker
* Clear contact paper/laminator
* Dry erase marker
* Paper towels

How to prepare the activity:

Cut a piece of poster board approximately 12" by 12". Draw a blank clock face on the poster paper, draw a blank space where each of the numbers 1-12 would be, and cover the clock face with clear contact paper. Place the blank clock face, a dry erase marker and some paper towels in the student's work area.

Activity:

The student will write the numbers 1-12 in the correct order on the blank clock face.

Part III:
Language/Reading Activities

Language Activity #1
ABC Train

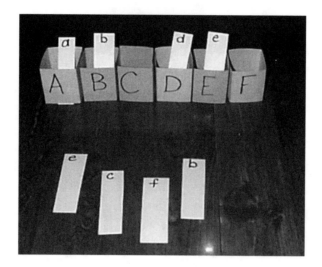

Objective:

Students will correctly match uppercase letters to lowercase letters. This activity will help students: identify the letters of the alphabet; reinforce the concept of upper and lower case letters.

What you will need:

* ❋ Twenty-six milk cartons (from the cafeteria)
* ❋ Index cards
* ❋ Marker
* ❋ Stapler

How to prepare the activity:

Cut the top off of all the milk cartons. Cut index cards to wrap around the index cards and staple them on securely. Next, staple all of the milk cartons together to resemble a train. Write the letters A-Z on each of the cartons. Using the index cards you have left, cut the cards in half, lengthwise. Write both lower- and uppercase letters on each of the cards. Place the "ABC Train" and the letter cards in front of the student.

Activity:

The student will place the letter cards in the corresponding milk cartons in the ABC train.

Language Activity #2
Writing/Tracing ABC's

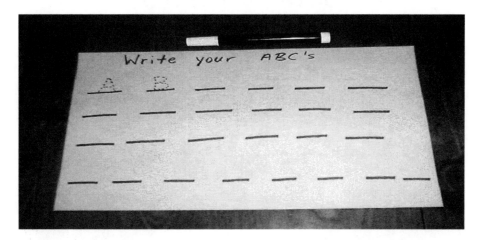

Objective:

Students will write the letters A-Z, in the correct order. This activity will help students: increase fine motor skills; reinforce the alphabet.

What you will need:

* Construction paper
* Clear contact paper/laminator
* Marker
* Dry erase marker
* Paper towels

How to prepare the activity:

Using the construction paper, draw 26 spaces. If the student has fine motor difficulty, then make another worksheet with the ABC's written on the page, so the student can practice tracing the letters. Cover the worksheet with clear contact paper. Place the worksheet, paper towels and a dry erase marker in the student's work area.

Activity:

The students will write/trace the letters in the spaces provided.

Language Activity #3
Sorting Upper/Lowercase Letters

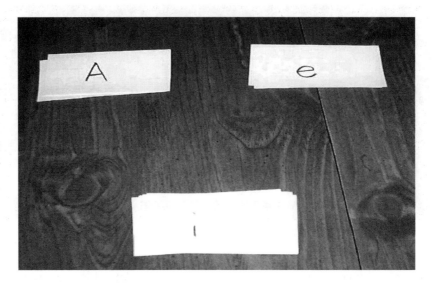

Objective:

Students will sort alphabet cards, by lowercase or uppercase, into the appropriate stack. This activity will help the student: discriminate between upper and lower case letters.

What you will need:

* Index cards
* Marker

How to prepare the activity:

Divide the index cards in half. Write an uppercase letter on each of the cards. Using the other half of the cards, write lowercase letters on each of the cards. Shuffle all of the cards and place the deck in the student's work area.

Activity:

The student will sort the index cards into two piles: one for uppercase and one for lowercase letters.

Language Activity #4
Sorting Word Cards

Objective:

Students will alphabetically sort word cards. This activity will help the student: visually discriminate between letters; perform simple alphabetizing tasks.

What you will need:

* Index cards
* Marker

How to prepare the activity:

Divide the index cards into four stacks. On the first stack, write words that begin with the letter "A." On the successive stacks, write words that begin with the letters "B," "C," and "D." Shuffle the cards and place in the student's work area.

Activity:

The student will sort the cards into four piles matching the first letter of each word.

Language Activity #5
Sequencing ABC's

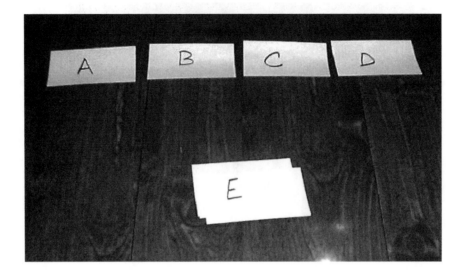

Objective:

Students will sequence letter cards alphabetically. This activity will help the student: reinforce the letters of the alphabet.

What you will need:

* Index cards (26)
* Marker

How to prepare the activity:

Write each of the letters A-Z on the index cards. Shuffle the stack of index cards and place the stack in the student's work area.

Activity:

The student will sequence the cards alphabetically.

Language Activity #6
Alphabetizing Word Cards

Objective:

Students will sort/alphabetize letter cards by their first letters. This activity will help the student: visually discriminate between letters; perform simple alphabetizing tasks.

What you will need:

* Index cards (26)
* Marker

How to prepare the activity:

Using the first index card, write a word beginning with the letter "A." On each of the successive cards, write a word beginning with the letters "B," "C," "D," etc. Shuffle the cards and place the deck in the student's work area.

Activity:

The student will sort/alphabetize the cards by their first letters.

Language Activity #7
Sorting Food Groups

Objective:

Students will sort food pictures by the food group to which they belong. This activity will help the student: perform simple sorting tasks; identify similarities and differences among objects; increase vocabulary skills.

What you will need:

* Food pictures (meat, dairy, fruits/vegetables and breads/cereals)
* Index cards (large size)
* Clear contact paper/laminator
* Sorting bins (4)

How to prepare the activity:

Cut out pictures of a variety of foods from magazines. Paste the pictures to large index cards and either laminate the pictures or cover the pictures with clear contact paper. Mix up all of the pictures and place them, along with four sorting bins in the student's work area. Label each of the bins with the name of a food group.

Activity:

The student will sort the pictures into the bins according to which food group they belong.

Language Activity #8
Sorting Transportation Pictures

Objective:

Students will sort transportation cards into the following stacks: Land, Air, or Water. This activity will help the student: perform simple sorting tasks; reinforce the concept of group; increase vocabulary skills.

What you will need:

* ✱ Transportation flash cards
* ✱ Sorting bins (3)

How to prepare the activity:

Mix up all of the cards and place the deck, along with three sorting bins in the student's work area. Label each of the bins either land, air or water.

Activity:

The student will sort the cards into the appropriate bins. Examples of "Land" pictures include the following: car, bicycle, truck, train, etc. Examples of "Air" pictures include the following: airplane, jet, helicopter, etc. Examples of "Water" pictures include the following: sailboat, tugboat, submarine, etc.

Language Activity #9
Sorting Clothing Pictures

Objective:

Students will sort clothing pictures by which part of the body they correspond to. This activity will help the student perform simple sorting tasks; reinforce the concept of group; increase vocabulary skills.

What you will need:

* Pictures of clothing items
* Sorting bins (5)

How to prepare the activity:

You can use pictures from magazines or flash cards. Shuffle the pictures and place them, along with the sorting bins, in the student's work area. Label each of the bins with a picture of where the clothing item will be placed on the body.

Activity:

The student will sort the cards into the bins according to where you wear it on your body.

For example, the following are items you wear on your head: hat, earmuffs, etc. Examples of items that you wear on your upper body include the following: shirt, jacket, vest, etc. Examples of items that you wear on your legs include the following: pants, shorts, skirts, etc. Items that you wear on you hands include the following: mittens, rings, etc. Examples of items that you wear on your feet include: shoes, socks, sandals, etc.

Language Activity #10
Sorting Object/Action Pictures

Objective:

Students will sort pictures by action or object. This activity will help the student: understand the concept of noun as an object; understand the concept of verb as an action.

What you will need:

* Various noun and verb pictures
* Sorting bins (2)

How to prepare the activity:

Cut out a variety of pictures of both objects and actions from magazines. Paste the pictures to large index cards and either laminate the pictures or cover the pictures with clear contact paper. Mix up all of the pictures and place them, along with two sorting bins in the student's work area. Label the bins –Noun Object and –Verb Action.

Activity:

The student will sort each card into the appropriate bin, according to whether it is a picture of an object or an action.

Language Activity #11
Sorting Boy/Girl Pictures

Objective:

Students will sort pictures by gender. This activity will help the students reinforce the concept of group;visually discriminate between boy and girl

What you will need:

* Pictures of boys and girls
* Sorting bins (2)

How to prepare the activity:

Cut out a variety of pictures of boys and girls from magazines. Paste the pictures to large index cards and either laminate the pictures or cover the pictures with clear contact paper. Mix up all of the pictures and place them, along with two sorting bins in the student's work area. Label the bins either boy or girl.

Activity:

The student will sort the cards according to whether they are pictures of boys or pictures of girl into the appropriate bins.

Language Activity #12
Sorting Man/Woman Pictures

Objective:

Students will sort pictures by gender. This activity will help the students reinforce the concept of a group; visually discriminate between man and women.

What you will need:

* Pictures of men and women
* Sorting bins (2)

How to prepare the activity:

Cut out a variety of pictures of men and women from magazines. Paste the pictures to large index cards and either laminate the pictures or cover the pictures with clear contact paper. Mix up all of the pictures and place them, along with two sorting bins in the student's work area. Label the bins either man or woman.

Activity:

The student will sort the cards according to whether they are pictures of men or pictures of women into the appropriate bins.

Language Activity #13
Matching Pictures to Restroom Signs

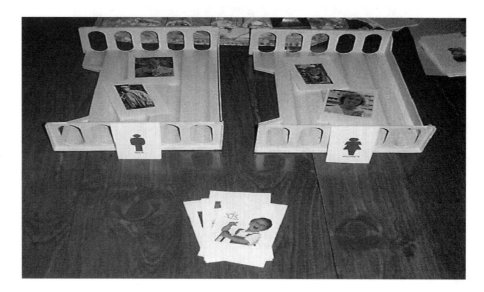

Objective:

Students will match gender pictures to the appropriately gendered restroom symbol. This activity will help the student: understand the relationship between symbols and people.

What you will need:

* Pictures of men, women, boys and girls
* Sorting bins (2)

How to prepare the activity:

Cut out a variety of pictures of men, women, boys and girls from magazines or use the pictures from Activities 11 and 12. Paste the pictures to large index cards and either laminate the pictures or cover the pictures with clear contact paper. Mix up all of the pictures and place them, along with two sorting bins in the student's work area. Label the bins with either the Male or Female Restroom Symbol.

Activity:

The student will sort the cards according to whether the person in the picture should go into the Male or the Female Restroom bin.

Language Activity #14
Sorting Food/Nonfood Pictures

Objective:

Students will sort pictures by either food or nonfood items. This activity will help the student: increase vocabulary; reinforce the concept of group.

What you will need:

* Pictures of food and nonfood items
* Sorting bins (2)

How to prepare the activity:

Cut out a variety of pictures of food and nonfood items from magazines. Paste the pictures to large index cards and either laminate the pictures or cover the pictures with clear contact paper. Mix up all of the pictures and place them, along with two sorting bins in the student's work area. Label the bins either food or nonfood items.

Activity:

The student will sort the cards according to whether they are pictures of men or pictures of women into the appropriate bins.

Language Activity #15
Sorting Clothing Items

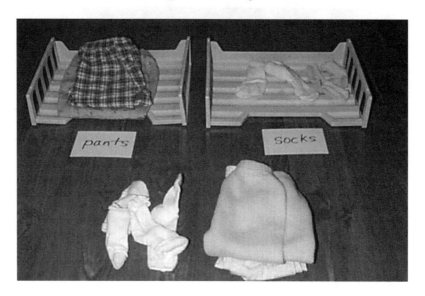

Objective:

Students will sort clothing items. This activity will help the student: discriminate between articles of clothing; reinforce the concept of group; and improve sorting skills.

What you will need:

 * Picture of a shirt, pants, shoes, socks and hat
 * Laundry basket
 * Shirts, pants, shoes, socks, and hats
 * Crates (5)

How to prepare the activity:

Stack the crates one on top of the other and tape one of each of the following pictures to the crates: shirt, pants, shoes, socks and hat. Place all of the various items of clothing into a laundry basket.

Activity:

The student will place each item of clothing into the crate labeled with that particular item of clothing.

Language Activity #16
Placing Word Cards on Objects

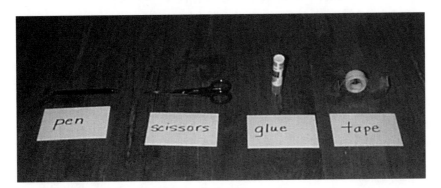

Objective:

Students will match word cards to the corresponding object. This activity will help the student: develop association between words and objects; increase sight word vocabulary.

What you will need:

- ✳ Index cards
- ✳ Marker
- ✳ Tape

How to prepare the activity:

Write the words on the index cards of objects commonly found in a classroom. Examples include the following: stapler, desk, chair, glue, globe, bookshelf, etc.

Activity:

The student will take each of the cards and tape it to the corresponding object found in the classroom.

Language Activity #17
Labeling Parts of the Body

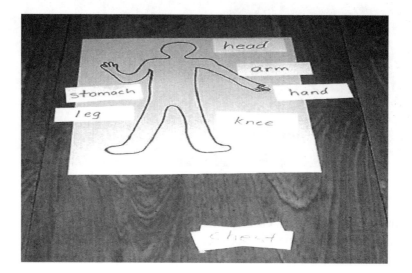

Objective:

Students will match body part word cards to the corresponding body part. This activity will help the student: associate names for parts of the body; increase sight vocabulary.

What you will need:

- ✳ Manila folder
- ✳ Marker
- ✳ Index cards
- ✳ Velcro

How to prepare the activity:

Draw an outline of the human body on the inside of a manila folder. Cut index cards into fourths, widthwise and write the following words on the small cards: head, neck, chest, stomach, arm, hand, leg, knee and foot. Place a piece of Velcro on the backs of the word cards and also in the area next to the corresponding parts of the body in the manila folder. Place the folder and the word cards in the student's work area.

Activity:

The student will match the words for the parts of the body with the corresponding part of the body in the manila folder.

Appendix

Part I:
Vocational Activity Mastery Checklists

MASTERY CHECKLIST

Part I: Vocational Activities
Matching Activities 1-7

Write in the date that the student masters each new skill.

Student's Name	Matching Number Cards	Matching Shape Cards	Pen Activity	Pencil/ Eraser Activity	Matching /Tying Shoelaces	Texture Matching Activity	Hook/ Washer Activity

MASTERY CHECKLIST

Part I: Vocational Activities
Sorting Activities 8-14

Write in the date that the student masters each new skill.

Student's Name	Sorting Beads	Sorting Silverware	Sorting Colored Paperclips	Construction Paper Activity	Recycling Activity	Sorting Numbers & Letters	Sorting Playing Cards

MASTERY CHECKLIST

Part I: Vocational Activities
Bundling Activities 15-19

Write in the date that the student masters each new skill.

Student's Name	Wrapping/ Bundling Flatware	Bundling Coffee Stirrers	Bundling Index Cards	Bundling Pencils	Bundling Pens

MASTERY CHECKLIST

Part I: Vocational Activities
Assembly Activities 20-22

Write in the date that the student masters each new skill.

Student's Name	Hardware Assembly	Ball-point pen Assembly	Flashlight Assembly

MASTERY CHECKLIST

Part I: Vocational Activities
Bagging/Packaging Activities 23-25

Write in the date that the student masters each new skill.

Student's Name	Bagging Flatware/ Condiments	Packaging Activity	Weighing/ Packaging Activity

MASTERY CHECKLIST

Part I: Vocational Activities
Various Clerical Activities 26-32

Write in the date that the student masters each new skill.

Student's Name	Folding Paper 1/3's with Envelopes	Stuffing Envelopes	Clipping Index Cards	Cross-Stacking Paper	Hole-punch Activity	Labeling Envelopes	Stamping Envelopes

MASTERY CHECKLIST

Part I: Vocational Activities
Various Clerical Activities 33-36

Write in the date that the student masters each new skill.

Student's Name	Stapling Activities	Taping Activity	Twine Activity	Paper Grid Activity

Part II:
Math Activities
Mastery Checklists

MASTERY CHECKLIST

Part II: Math Activities
Money Activities: 1-8

Write in the date that the student masters each new skill.

Student's Name	Coin Matching	Penny Counting	Nickel Counting	Dime Counting	Quarter Counting	Sorting Paper Money	Sorting Plastic Coins	Money Bingo

MASTERY CHECKLIST

Part II: Math Activities
Counting Activities: 9-17

Write in the date that the student masters each new skill.

Student's Name	Sequencing Number Cards	Matching Number Cards	Sequencing Set Cards	Counting Activity	Writing/ Tracing Activity	Writing By 5's	Writing by 10's	Sequencing By 5's	Sequencing By 10's

MASTERY CHECKLIST

Part II: Math Activities
Various Math Activities: 8-21

Write in the date that the student masters each new skill.

Student's Name	Sorting by Place Value	Adding Train	Clock Face Activity	Writing On Clock Face

Part III:
Language/Reading Activities
Mastery Checklists

MASTERY CHECKLIST

Part III: Language Activities
Alphabet Activities: 1-6

Write in the date that the student masters each new skill.

Student's Name	ABC Train	Writing/ Tracing ABC's	Sorting Upper/ Lowercase Letters	Sorting Word Cards	Sequencing ABC's	Alpha- Betizing Word Cards

MASTERY CHECKLIST

Part III: Language Activities
Language Activities: 7-14

Write in the date that the student masters each new skill.

Student's Name	Sorting Food Groups	Sorting Trans-Portation Pictures	Sorting Clothing Pictures	Sorting Object/ Action Pictures	Sorting Boy/Girl Pictures	Sorting Man/ Woman Pictures	Matching Pics to Restroom Signs	Sorting Food/ Nonfood Items

MASTERY CHECKLIST

Part III: Language Activities
Language Activities: 15-17

Write in the date that the student masters each new skill.

Student's Name	Sorting Clothing Items	Placing Word Cards On Objects	Labeling Parts Of the Body

About the Author

Beverly Thorne, B.S. Ed., a special education teacher, has had experience teaching students with the following exceptionalities: autism, moderate to severe mental retardation, behavioral/emotional disorder, and hearing impairment. She had been working in a private residential school for students with severe behavioral disorders when she decided to take time off to raise her first child and write this book, *Hands-On Activities for Exceptional Children.*

Inclusion: Strategies for Working with Young Children Lorraine O. Moore, Ph.D.
A gold mine of developmentally based ideas to help children between the ages of 3-7 or older students who are developmentally delayed. This book commences with a synopsis of inclusive education and the future of learning. Subsequent chapters present hundreds of child focused strategies. Communication, large and small motor development, pre-reading, writing and math are only a few of the topics covered. Reproducible activities help children learn about feelings, empathy, resolving conflicts peacefully and problem solving. Reproducible forms help to chart students' rate and frequency of behaviors, modifications, child interview and more! P301 / $23.95 / 192 pages / soft cover

Life Skill Activities for Special Children Darlene Mannix
Educators (grades 3-8) will find 145 ready-to-use uniformly formatted lessons to introduce and reinforce basic survival skills, self-care skills, community independence, and the ability to get along with others. Each activity provides step-by-step directions, teaching suggestions, learning objectives, and answer keys. Reproducible activity sheets. PH 208 / $29.95 / 368 pages / soft cover

Ready-to-Use Lessons & Activities for the Inclusive Primary Classroom
Eileen Kennedy
This publication is for educators (grades K-3). This book includes 122 lessons with reproducible pages that cover social skills, communications, arts, math science, social studies, physical education and health. Each lesson includes class objectives for use with the entire class as well as individual performance objectives and projects that can be used with individual students. PH102 / $34.95 / 350 pages / soft cover

Social Skills Activities for Special Children Darlene Mannix
Educators (grades 2-6) will find 142 ready-to-use lessons and reproducible master activity sheets to help students become aware of acceptable social behavior and develop proficiency in acquiring basic social skills both inside and outside of the classroom. Stories, lessons, and 140 hands-on activities help students to accept rules and authority at school, relate to peers and develop positive social skills.
PH 207 /$29.95 / 416 pages / soft cover

Life Skills Activities for Secondary Students with Special Needs Darlene Mannix
This excellent publication provides educators (grades 7-12) with 190 step-by-step lessons and reproducible activity sheets to help students develop and practice the basic "survival" skills needed for both school and daily living situations. Help your students develop skills in the following areas: academic, interpersonal skills, communication, practical living, vocational, lifestyle choices, and problem solving. PH 206 / $29.95 / 510 pages

Social Skills Activities for Secondary Students with Special Needs
Darlene Mannix
This resource for educators (grades 8-12) and counselors prides a flexible activities based program to help secondary students learn and internalize appropriate ways to behave around others. The activities help students gain control over situations by actively contributing to the social outcome. The 187 ready-to-use worksheets are organized into two sections: Social Skills that are Helpful and Necessary, and Social Skills in Action. The lessons can easily adapted for entire classes, individuals or may be used in small group settings. PH 203 / $29.95 / 352 pages

Life Skills Development Series
This comprehensive program is developed for secondary students with developmental disabilities. Each program offers life skill curricula and hands-on materials necessary to acquire the targeted skills. Curricula covers the following areas: personal hygiene; housekeeping; grocery and clothes shopping; cooking healthy foods; dining out in several types of restaurants and scheduling. All curricula provide objectives, training suggestions, potential problems and task analysis. Thousand of hands-on materials; shopping cards; picture-sequenced cookbook; personal care cards; dining and scheduling cards are included. Appointment and pocket books are provided so Cards may be taken on outings. Each set includes a 100 + page guide. The programs may be ordered individually or as a set.
AT201 Keeping the House Curriculum Set / $89.95
AT202 Looking Good Curriculum Set / $89.95
AT203 Plan Your Day Curriculum Set / $89.95
AT204 Shopping Smart / $89.95
The following two should be ordered together.
AT205 Home Cooking Curriculum / $89.95
AT206 Select-A-Meal Curriculum / $89.95

AT200Set All five programs in the Life Skills Development Series.

Resources for Curriculum Support
Available from Peytral Publications, Inc.

Hands-On Phonics Activities for Elementary Children Karen Meyers Stangl
Classroom teachers and specialists will find hundreds of stimulating hands-on activities for developing children's knowledge of the alphabet and letter-sound relationship, plus scores of reproducible book and work lists that can be used to tailor almost any of the activities in the book to a specific phonics skill. This exceptional new book is organized into three section: Phonics Activities for Pre-Readers (K-1); Activities for Emerging Readers (Grades 1-2); Activities for Developing Readers (Grades 2-5); and lists fro developing Hands-On Phonics Activities. Also included are reproducible game boards, Alphabet Mini Flash Cards and a Phonics Assessment Profile that can be used to chart each child's progress.   PH301 / $27.95 / 368 pages

Phonemic Awareness: Lessons, Activities and Games Victoria Groves Scott.
For many students, Phonemic Awareness Training is the key to open the door to reading. If you teach students who encounter difficulty hearing subtle differences in words such as "pen" and "pin", experience difficulty rhyming words, blending sounds in isolation or who consistently substitute sounds like "chrain" for "train" phonemic awareness training may be the missing component to help these struggling students. In as little as 20 minutes a day, this training may be incorporated as a prerequisite or supplement to any reading program. This book includes an overview of phonemic awareness principles, 48 scripted lesson – ready for immediate use, 49 reproducible blackline masters and progress charts. In the companion video **Phonemic Awareness: The Sounds of Reading**, Dr. Scott demonstrates the principle components of phonemic awareness training: identification, comparison, segmentation, blending, and rhyming. She guides the viewer through practical lessons designed for both elementary and special education teachers. Dr. Scott has had great success using phonemic awareness training not only with K-3 students but also with middle school students who have struggled with reading.
P603 / Phonemic Awareness Book and Staff Development video / $79.95
P600 / Phonemic Awareness: Lessons, Activities and Games / $29.95 / 176 pages

Teaching Reading to Children with Down Syndrome: A Guide for Parents and Teachers
Patricia Logan Oelwein
This nationally known reading program ensures success by presenting lessons which are both imaginative and functional and can be tailored to meet the needs of each student. This publication includes 100 pages of reproducible materials to supplement the program. Although developed for students with Down Syndrome this guide will help many struggling students learn to read. WP104 / $18.95 / 370 pages